D0116883

Armadillo's Burrow

by Dee Phillips

Consultants:

Dr. Colleen McDonough
IUCN/SSC Anteater, Sloth & Armadillo Specialist Group

Kimberly Brenneman, PhD
National Institute for Early Education Research, Rutgers University, New Brunswick, New Jersey

BEARPORT PUBLISHING

New York, New York

Credits
Cover, © Wayne Lynch/All Canada Photos/Superstock and © Ng Yin Jian/Shutterstock; 4, © Charlie Bittner; 5, 6T, © Martha Marks/Shutterstock; 6B, © Cosmographics; 7, © Norbert Wu/Minden Pictures/FLPA; 8, © Wayne Lynch/All Canada Photos/Superstock; 9, © Dhoxax/Shutterstock, © Lev Kropotov/Shutterstock, and © Heiko Kiera/Shutterstock; 10–11, © Animals Animals/Superstock; 12, © age fotostock/Superstock; 13, © Pan Xunbin/Shutterstock, © D. Kucharski & K. Kucharska/Shutterstock, © Wong Hock weng/Shutterstock, © Sergey Goruppa/Shutterstock, and © Africa Studio/Shutterstock; 14, © Cynthia Kidwell/Shutterstock, © Contessa/Shutterstock, © Nagel Photography/Shutterstock, and © Eric Isselee/Shutterstock; 15, © Bianca Lavies/National Geographic Stock; 16–17, © Bianca Lavies/Getty Images; 18–19, © Bianca Lavies/National Geographic Stock; 20, © Martin Harvey/Getty Images; 21, © Animals Animals/Superstock; 22, © John Young, © Pedro Vidal/Shutterstock, © Hhsu/Shutterstock, and © pittaya/Shutterstock; 23TL, © Martha Marks/Shutterstock; 23TC, © Charlie Bittner; 23TR, © FocalPoint/Shutterstock; 23BL, © SA Team/FN/Minden Pictures/FLPA; 23BC, © 2009fotofriends/Shutterstock; 23BR, © Heiko Kiera/Shutterstock.

Publisher: Kenn Goin
Editorial Director: Adam Siegel
Editor: Joy Bean
Creative Director: Spencer Brinker
Design: Alix Wood
Editor: Mark J. Sachner
Photo Researcher: Ruby Tuesday Books Ltd

Library of Congress Cataloging-in-Publication Data in process at time of publication (2013)
Library of Congress Control Number: 2012040427 5-045-4098 3/13
ISBN-13: 978-1-61772-746-7 (library binding)

For more information, write to Bearport Publishing Company, Inc., 45 West 21st Street, Suite 3B, New York, New York 10010. Printed in the United States of America.

10 9 8 7 6 5 4 3 2 1

Contents

An Armadillo's New Home

It's a warm, summer evening in a forest.

Hidden under a tree is a hole surrounded by loose soil.

Suddenly, a very unusual-looking creature backs out of the hole.

The animal is a nine-banded armadillo, and the hole is the entrance to its **burrow**.

Deep underground, the busy armadillo has been digging a new home!

entrance hole

nine-banded armadillo

loose soil

Armadillos sleep and raise their babies in their burrows.

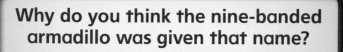

Why do you think the nine-banded armadillo was given that name?

Check Out an Armadillo

Armadillos have bodies covered in sections of bony **armor** called plates.

The plates are covered in tough, leathery skin that is made up of small **scales**.

Nine-banded armadillos usually have nine bands of scaly armor on their backs.

They live in places that are warm all year round.

Some of these animals live in forests, while others live on open, grassy **prairies**.

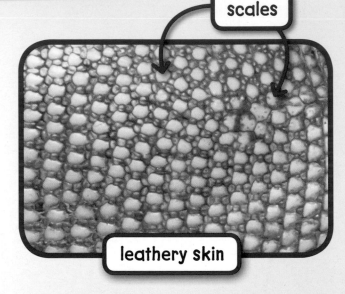

scales

leathery skin

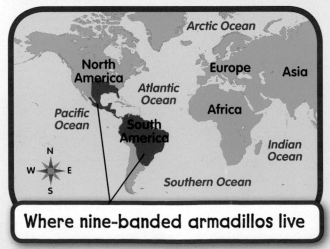

Arctic Ocean

North America

Europe

Asia

Atlantic Ocean

Pacific Ocean

South America

Africa

Indian Ocean

Southern Ocean

N
W E
S

Where nine-banded armadillos live

Welcome to an Armadillo's Burrow

An armadillo begins work on a burrow by digging an entrance hole.

It digs and loosens the soil with the long claws on its front feet.

It also uses its long nose, or snout, to break up the soil.

Then it uses its back feet to kick the soil out of the hole.

The armadillo digs until the tunnel is up to 13 feet (4 m) long.

At the end of the tunnel, it digs a bedroom to sleep in.

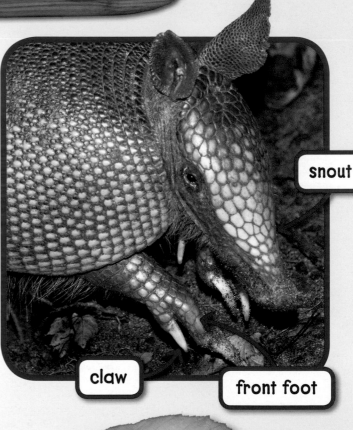

snout

claw

front foot

Armadillos have four claws on each front foot and five claws on each back foot.

forest

burrow
entrance

tunnel

bedroom

An Armadillo's Day and Night

An armadillo may dig up to 12 burrows in the area where it lives.

During the day it sleeps in one of its underground homes.

When evening comes, it wakes up and leaves its burrow.

It spends the night wandering slowly around its home area looking for food.

In the morning, it finds one of its burrows and goes back underground to sleep.

an armadillo leaving its burrow to find food

An armadillo's cozy bedroom may be up to 6 feet (1.8 m) underground.

Guess what types of food an armadillo eats. How do you think it finds its food?

Digging for Dinner

An armadillo's main food is **insects** such as beetles, termites, and ants.

It eats adult insects and baby insects called grubs.

These small animals often live belowground or under leaves that have fallen from trees.

An armadillo uses its nose and claws to dig in leaves and soil to find its food.

How do you think armadillos stay safe from enemies when they are not underground?

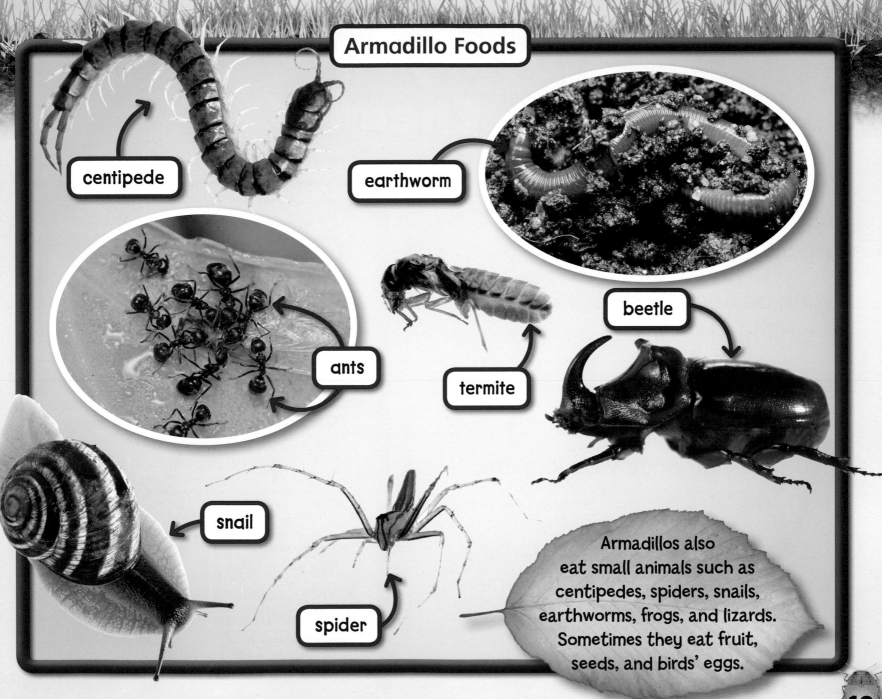

Armadillo Foods

centipede

earthworm

ants

termite

beetle

snail

spider

Armadillos also eat small animals such as centipedes, spiders, snails, earthworms, frogs, and lizards. Sometimes they eat fruit, seeds, and birds' eggs.

13

Staying Safe from Enemies

Large enemies sometimes attack armadillos.

When an enemy comes close, an armadillo hides inside a burrow.

If it is not near a burrow, an armadillo has a great trick.

It surprises an enemy by leaping up in the air.

The enemy isn't sure what to do next, and the armadillo has time to escape unharmed.

Armadillo Enemies

coyote

puma

pet dog

bear

An armadillo's tough armor protects its body if an enemy tries to bite or scratch it.

a leaping armadillo

A Burrow for Babies

Adult armadillos usually live alone.

In the summer, however, males and females meet up and **mate**.

Then, early the next spring, each female armadillo that mated digs a new burrow.

She makes a soft nest of grass in the burrow's bedroom.

Then, safe in her underground home, she gives birth to four babies, called pups.

Right away, she begins to feed them milk from her body.

A newborn armadillo pup weighs about 2.5 ounces (71 g). Pick up a tennis ball and feel its weight. The baby armadillo weighs about the same as the ball.

A female armadillo uses her front legs to carry leaves and grass to her burrow. She hops backward on her two back legs to get home.

mother armadillo

pups drinking milk

Armadillo Pups

A newborn armadillo pup looks just like an adult, but it is much smaller.

The pup's armor plates are soft and bendable, though, like shoe leather.

The pup's armor will slowly harden during the first 12 weeks of its life.

Armadillo pups stay underground until they are about three to four weeks old.

Then they begin to leave the burrow in the early evening.

While their mother goes to find food, the pups spend time aboveground.

A female armadillo's four pups will be either four girls or four boys. The babies are never a mix of boys and girls.

Draw an armadillo pup. Then label as many of the pup's body parts as you can.

three-week-old armadillo pups

The Pups Grow Up

At five weeks old, armadillo pups start to eat insects and other adult foods.

They still drink their mother's milk, however, until they are about 12 weeks old.

When fall comes, the pups are ready to leave their mother.

They know how to dig burrows and how to search for food.

Each young armadillo goes off on its own to begin its adult life.

armadillo pups digging for food

An armadillo is fully grown at about two years old. By then it will weigh about 10 pounds (4.5 kg).

a 6-week-old armadillo pup

Science Lab

Be an Armadillo Scientist

When scientists study animals, they sometimes search for footprints.

Look at the photos of the four footprints on this page.

Which footprint do you think was made by an armadillo's front foot?

You can look at the feet of the armadillos in this book to help you decide.

Now check your answer on page 24.

The armadillo footprint in the photo is life-size.

Measure the footprint with a ruler. How long is it?

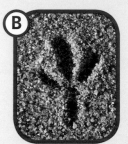
A

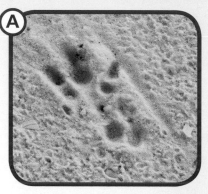
B

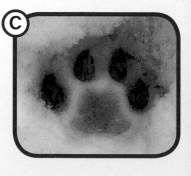
C

D

Science Words

armor (AR-mur) a covering that protects the body

burrow (BUR-oh) a hole or tunnel dug by an animal to live in

insects (IN-sekts) small animals that have six legs, an exoskeleton, two antennas, and three main body parts

mate (MAYT) to come together in order to have young

prairies (PRAIR-eez) large areas of flat land covered with grass

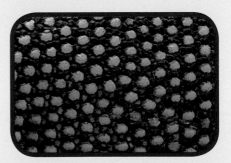

scales (SKALEZ) small pieces of hard skin that cover the body of an animal

23

Index

Read More

McKerley, Jennifer Guess. *Amazing Armadillos (Step into Reading).* New York: Random House Children's Books (2009).

Sebastian, Emily. *Armadillos (Animals Underground).* New York: PowerKids Press (2012).

Townsend, Emily Rose. *Armadillos (Desert Animals).* Mankato, MN: Capstone (2004).

Learn More Online

To learn more about armadillos, visit **www.bearportpublishing.com/TheHoleTruth!**

Answers

Answers to the activity on page 22

- A is an armadillo's foot
- B is a bird's foot
- C is a cat's foot
- D is a dog's foot

About the Author

Dee Phillips lives near the ocean on the southwest coast of England. She writes nonfiction and fiction books for children. Dee's biggest ambition is to one day walk the entire coast of Britain—it will take about ten months!